W9-AYR-639

LF

THE HUMAN BODY

THE NERVOUS SYSTEM

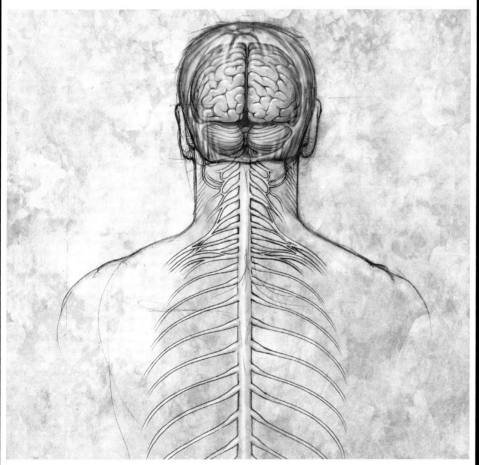

By Susan H. Gray

THE CHILD'S WORLD®
CHANHASSEN, MINNESOTA

Published in the United States of America by the Child's World®
P.O. Box 326, Chanhassen, MN 55317-0326
800-599-READ
www.childsworld.com

Subject adviser:
R. John Solaro, Ph.D.,
Distinguished
University Professor
and Head, Department
of Physiology and
Biophysics, University
of Illinois Chicago,
Chicago, Illinois

Photo Credits: Cover: Artville/Scott Bodell; Bettmann/Corbis: 18; Corbis: 9, 11 (Ron Boardman; Frank Lane Picture Agency), 14 (Ariel Skelley), 19 (Jose Luiz Pelaez Inc.), 22 (Reuters NewMedia Inc.), 27 (Roy Morsch); Custom Medical Stock Pictures: 6, 7, 8, 12, 13, 15, 16, 17, 23, 25; PhotoEdit: 5 (Michael Newman), 10 (Spencer Grant), 20 (Deborah Davis), 21 (Patrick Olear), 24 (Richard Hutchings), 26 (Mark Richards).

The Child's World®: Mary Berendes, Publishing Director

Editorial Directions, Inc.: E. Russell Primm, Editorial Director; Elizabeth K. Martin, Line Editor; Katie Marsico, Assistant Editor; Olivia Nellums, Editorial Assistant; Susan Hindman, Copy Editor; Elizabeth K. Martin, Proofreader; Peter Garnham, Marilyn Mallin, Mary Hoffman, Fact Checkers; Tim Griffin/IndexServ, Indexer; Cian Loughlin O'Day, Photo Researcher; Linda S. Koutris, Photo Selector

Library of Congress Cataloging-in-Publication Data
Gray, Susan Heinrichs.
  The nervous system / by Susan H. Gray.
    p. cm. — (Living well)
Includes bibliographical references and index.
Contents: What is the nervous system?—What is a nerve cell?—How does the nervous system work?—What about the senses?
  ISBN 1-59296-039-1 (lib. bdg. : alk. paper)
  1. Nervous system—Juvenile literature. [1. Nervous system.] I. Title. II. Series: Living well (Child's World (Firm)
  QM351.G73 2004
  612.8—dc21   2003006291

TABLE OF CONTENTS

CHAPTER ONE

BLASTING AWAY

Michael was really hot. Today, he was beating *everybody* at video games. His eyes darted back and forth. He missed nothing on the screen. His fingers were wrapped tightly around the controller. He punched its button with a sharp jab. An asteroid blasted out of the sky.

Another asteroid popped up on the screen. Special nerve cells in Michael's eyes spotted it. Other cells picked up its bright blue color. The cells shot a message to Michael's brain: "There's something on the screen!" In the brain, other cells got the signal: "It's an asteroid! Blast it!" They zoomed the signal down Michael's neck and out to his arm. Muscles in his thumb got the message. Michael punched the controller button. The asteroid blew to bits.

Everything happened in a split second. Michael's thumb jabbed the button almost as soon as his eyes saw the asteroid. His nerves and muscles worked together. They reacted in a flash. And Michael racked up another 500 points.

Michael's nervous system helped him react quickly to blast asteroids.

CHAPTER TWO

WHAT IS THE NERVOUS SYSTEM?

T he nervous system is the body's "wiring." It is a network of cells reaching throughout the whole body. Special

parts of the cells sense things in the **environment.** They pick up light, sound, touch **pressure,** and temperature, for example. Other parts of the cells cause the body to react. They make you blink, grin, and press a controller button.

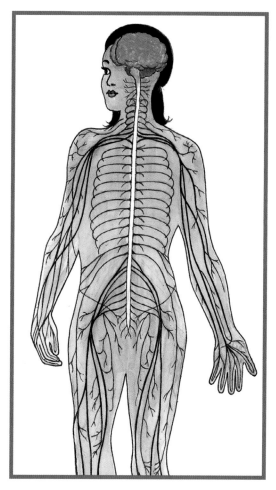

The nervous system includes the brain, the spinal cord, and nerve cells going to all parts of the body.

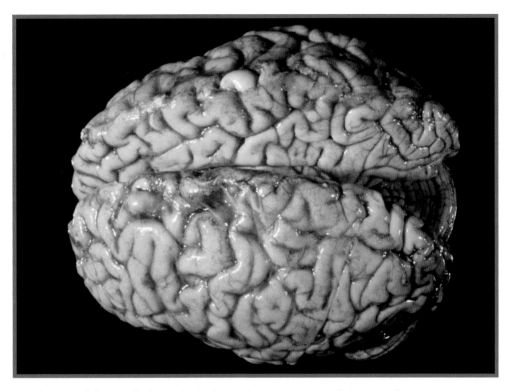

A mass of tissue cells form the brain, an important part of the central nervous system

The nervous system is made up of two parts. They are the central

nervous system and the peripheral (pur-IF-urh-uhl) nervous system.

The central nervous system includes the brain and the spinal cord.

The brain is a soft mass of nerve tissue in the skull. In an adult, it

weighs about 3 pounds (1.36 kilograms). The spinal cord is a bundle

of nerve cells. It starts at the base of the brain and runs down the back. Bones of the back surround and protect it. In an adult, the spinal cord is about 18 inches (46 centimeters) long.

The peripheral nervous system is made up of all the other nerves throughout the body. It includes nerves running from the ears to the brain. It includes nerves going from the spinal cord out to the finger-tips. It even includes nerves that lead to the heart and lungs.

People can control the actions of some nerves. Actions you can control are called voluntary (VOLL-uhn-TEHR-ee) actions. For instance, you can control the nerves that make your

Nerves leading to the lungs, shown on this digital X ray in red, keep you breathing without having to think about it.

When you decide to chew gum, your nervous system turns your thought into an action.

legs run. You can also control the nerves that make your mouth

chew gum. Your brain can decide to do these things. Then your

nervous system makes them happen.

Some of the body's activities happen automatically. These are

called involuntary actions. You do not have to think about these

The nervous system keeps your body working, even as you sleep.

activities for them to happen. But the nervous system still controls

them. For example, you don't have to lie awake at night, remembering

to breathe. You don't have to remind your **intestines** to push food

along. Nerves to the lungs and intestines just take care of these things.

CHAPTER THREE

WHAT IS A NERVE CELL?

The nervous system is made up of millions of nerve cells.

Nerve cells are also called neurons (NUHR-awnz). Some neurons are very short. They might run only from one part of the brain to another. Other neurons are much longer. These might run from the spinal cord all the way down to the toes.

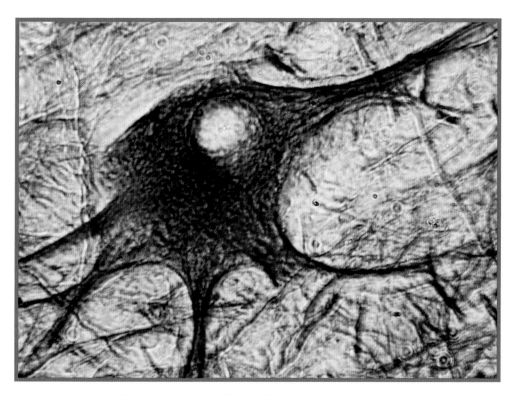

Neurons, or nerve cells, can be very long or very short.
These neurons are found in the spinal cord.

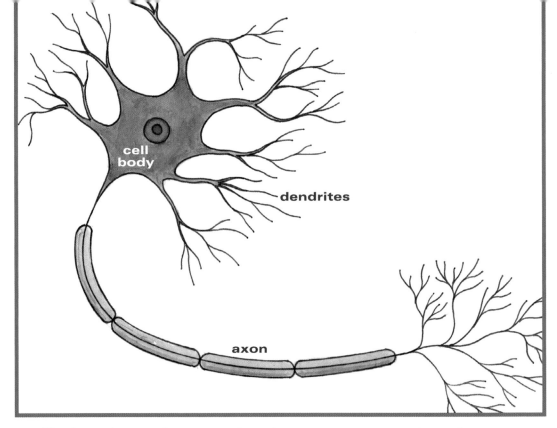

The three main parts of a neuron work together to pass messages to muscles or other neurons.

A nerve cell, or neuron, has three main parts. They are the dendrites (DEN-drites), the cell body, and the axon (AX-on). Most nerve cells have several dendrites. These are short, little hairlike branches. They lead to the cell body. The cell body is an enlarged part of the neuron. It is often star-shaped. An axon extends from the cell body. In many neurons, the axon runs out to end right at the muscle cells. In others, the axon meets dendrites of another neuron.

CHAPTER FOUR

HOW DOES THE NERVOUS SYSTEM WORK?

The nervous system works by picking up messages and

making the body respond. Some messages go to the brain.

Other messages leave from the brain. Nerves in your hand might send

a message to the brain when they sense a pin prick. Your brain would

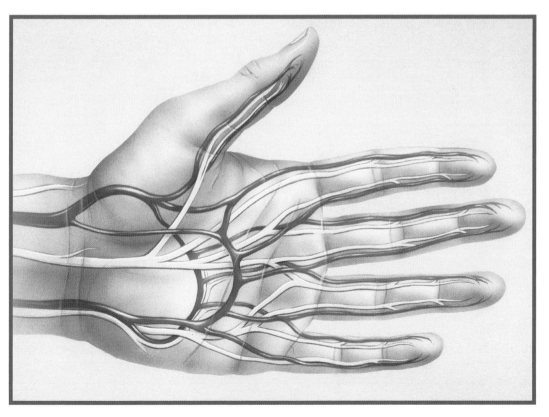

*The main nerves of the hand, shown in yellow, pass through
the wrist and branch out to each finger.*

Nerve endings in your nose and eyes help you enjoy the smell and colors of a beautiful flower.

send out a message telling the mouth to say "Ouch!" Nerve endings in

the skin, eyes, ears, nose, and tongue pick up messages. Nerve endings

deep inside the body also pick up messages.

First, the dendrites pick up

the signals. The ends of some

dendrites are built to pick

up heat, cold, or touch.

Some are built to pick up

light, color, sound, smell, or taste.

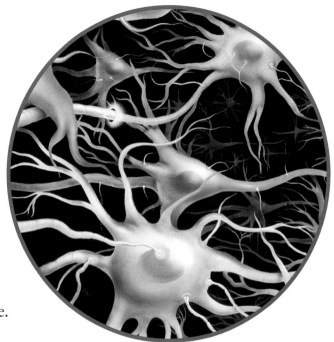

Then dendrites send their signals

This drawing shows how the axons and dendrites of neurons connect with each other.

to the cell body and axon. They send these signals as electricity.

The electricity speeds down the axon to the central nervous system.

In the central nervous system, other nerves translate the messages.

They figure out what the messages mean and how the body should

react. The brain or spinal cord then shoots electrical signals down

other nerves. These signals zoom out to body parts, telling them what

to do. The nerve endings release chemicals at these body parts. The chemicals can make muscles move. They can make you jump away from danger. They can make you punch a controller button.

When Michael blew away the asteroid, his eyes, brain, spinal cord, nerves, and muscles all worked together. It took electricity and chemicals for everything to happen. And it all took place in a flash.

In many cases, the nerve signals pass through the brain and spinal cord. But in some cases, they only pass through the spinal cord.

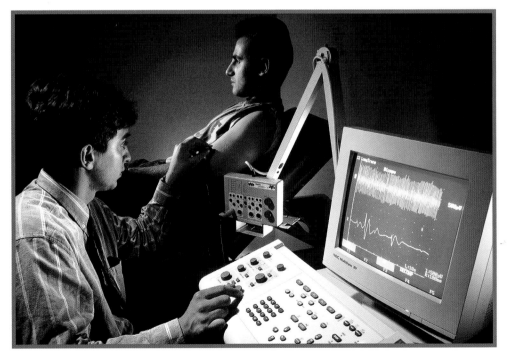

A doctor tests how quickly this man's muscles can react to different signals.

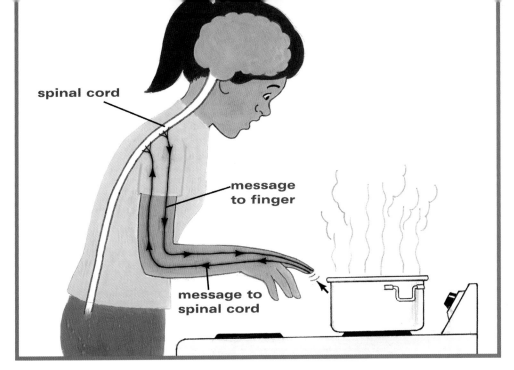

Reflex pathways from the spinal cord to the muscles help us respond quickly to danger.

Nerves that only go to the spinal cord are called the reflex pathways.

Reflexes help us in times of danger.

Suppose you touch a hot iron. Suddenly your hand jerks back.

Here, nerves in your fingers sent signals to the spinal cord. Then

nerves in the spinal cord sent signals right to your arm. They made

your arm and hand pull away from danger. The signals did not have

to travel all the way to the brain. This allowed you to escape danger

more quickly.

More than 2,000 years ago, a Greek thinker named Aristotle (below) had some ideas about nerves. He believed the heart controlled them. Hundreds of years later, a Roman doctor named Galen had his own ideas. He believed that the brain controlled the nerves. But he thought the nerves were hollow tubes. He said that a person's "animal spirit" flowed through the tubes. The spirit caused the person to sense things and to move.

For nearly a thousand years, scientists were stuck on the idea of animal spirits. Their ideas began to change in the 1700s. Maybe, they said, electrical signals ran through nerves. In the 1920s, a man named Otto Loewi discovered nerve chemicals. By then, many centuries had passed since Aristotle's time. But scientists finally had the right idea.

CHAPTER FIVE

WHAT ABOUT THE SENSES?

People have five senses. These are sight, hearing, smell, taste, and touch. Senses tell us about the environment around us. The body has special nerve cells that pick up information about the environment. Many of these cells are in the eyes, ears, nose, and tongue. Many more are in the skin, where they pick up pressure.

Nerve cells in his ears let this boy hear the song his grandmother is playing.
Nerve cells in the skin on her fingers allow her to feel the guitar strings.

Many people who are colorblind have trouble seeing red and green tones.

More than 100 million special cells in the eyes pick up light and color. They send pictures to the brain. Neurons in the brain figure out the meanings of the pictures. Some of the eye cells pick up different colors. People who are colorblind are often missing some of these eye cells. They cannot tell the difference between certain colors. Usually they cannot see red or green. About one boy in 12 is colorblind.

But only about one girl in 200 has this problem.

Cells deep inside the ear pick up vibrations from sound waves.

They send the vibrations to the brain. The brain sorts out their

meanings. People with ear infections cannot hear well. This is often

because the **passage** through the ear is swollen. Sound waves

cannot reach the cells.

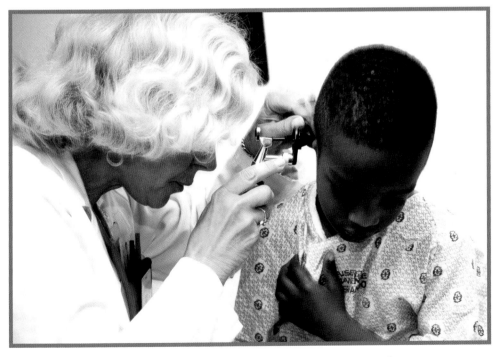

An ear infection blocks sound from getting to nerve cells
inside your ear, making it hard to hear.

Cells in the nose pick up different smells. Actually, they are picking up chemicals in the air. The brain interprets the chemical messages. Human beings have 40 million nose cells doing this job. But some dogs have more than a *billion!*

Taste buds in the tongue also pick up chemicals. Taste buds are little onion-shaped bundles of cells. They can only be seen with a microscope. The average person has several thousand taste buds.

This dog is helping find people buried after an earthquake by using his amazing sense of smell.

Hundreds of little bumps cover the tongue. These bumps are called papillae (puh-PILL-ee). Taste buds lie along the sides and bottoms of papillae (right). Taste buds detect the different chemicals that give food its flavor. About one person in four has many more papillae and taste buds than normal. These people taste things very strongly. Scientists call them "super tasters."

Because their sense of taste is so strong, some foods taste absolutely terrible. Many super tasters cannot stand to eat bitter foods such as broccoli, Brussels sprouts, or grapefruit. Taco sauce just burns them up. And very salty foods are sickening.

However, a few super tasters have put this problem to good use. They have learned to identify all the different tastes in foods. For instance, they can eat a piece of pie and tell what spices are in it. They might even know what was used to make the crust. These people sometimes work for food companies. They try out new foods, such as cereal, canned soup, and pudding. If they do not like a food, they can tell the cooks exactly what is wrong. If they do like it, companies know that most other people will like it, too.

CHAPTER SIX

KEEPING THE NERVOUS SYSTEM HEALTHY

The nervous system works properly in most people. This is because it gets plenty of **oxygen** from the blood. It also gets the proper **nutrients.** Foods such as chicken and fish contain the protein needed to make nerve chemicals. Bread, pasta, and fruit provide the sugar for energy. And vitamin B^{12}, found in eggs and milk, helps to build and strengthen the nerve cells.

The protein found in fish and milk helps keep your nervous system running well.

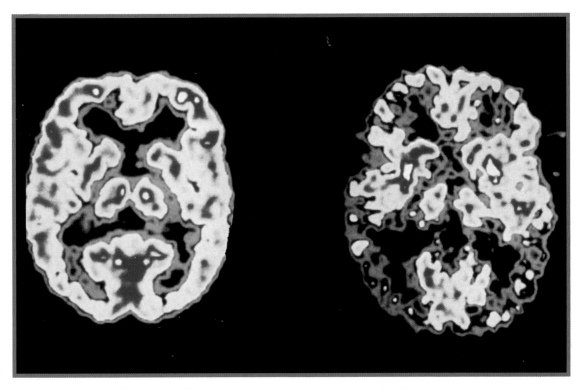

*The scan on the right shows how the brain of an Alzheimer's patient
has less activity than a normal brain, shown on the left.*

Some diseases keep the nervous system from doing its job.

Alzheimer's disease often affects older people. They begin to have

trouble remembering simple facts. Over time, they may not be able

to make decisions or even recognize their own family members.

Some scientists think Alzheimer's may be caused by clumps called

tangles inside the brain's neurons. Other scientists are looking at

People with Alzheimer's disease often feel confused and cannot recognize even people they know well.

how diet, environment, or viruses might cause the disease. They still have many questions about Alzheimer's. But scientists think that keeping your mind and body active for your whole life may help you avoid this disease.

A blood clot in the brain can also cause serious problems for the nervous system. The clot keeps blood from getting to the nerve cells. The cells then fail to get enough oxygen or nutrients. After a few minutes, neurons start to die. If certain neurons die, a person may forget where he lives. If others die, he could lose his sense of smell.

If still others die, he could have trouble moving or talking. When

oxygen and nutrients cannot reach brain cells, a person is said to

have a stroke.

Usually the nervous system works properly, though. Every second,

it shoots messages all over the body. It stays busy without us knowing,

even as we sleep. The system is truly amazing.

A healthy nervous system allows you to experience all the sights,
sounds, smells, and tastes of our world.

Glossary

detect (di-TEKT) To detect something is to discover or sense it.

environment (en-VYE-ruhn-muhnt) The environment is the things that surround a living creature.

intestines (in-TESS-tinz) Intestines are the long, tubelike part of the digestive system.

nutrients (NOO-tree-uhnts) Nutrients are the things found in foods that are needed for life and health.

oxygen (OK-suh-juhn) Oxygen is a gas in the air that humans need to breathe.

passage (PASS-ij) A passage is a pathway.

pressure (PRESH-ur) Pressure is the force caused by pressing.

Questions and Answers about the Nervous System

How many neurons are there in the brain? No one is quite sure how many neurons are in the brain. Experts believe the number is somewhere between 10 billion and 100 billion.

What are the longest neurons in the body? The longest nerves are the two sciatic (sy-AT-ik) nerves. They run from the spinal cord, down the back of each leg. Then they split and run down to the feet.

What does caffeine do to the nervous system? Caffeine interferes with a natural chemical in the brain that slows down the activity of neurons. When you drink a soft drink with caffeine in it, the neurons speed up instead of slowing down! Your heart starts beating faster and your muscles tighten up. Caffeine also makes it difficult to sleep. If you keep drinking or eating things with caffeine, your body starts to depend on it. It is best to limit the amount of caffeine your body takes in each day.

Did You Know?

- Some people are born with a nervous system that does not detect pain. As they grow up, they get cuts, scratches, and broken bones, and they don't even know it.

- Children have far more nerve cells in their brains than grown-ups do. As people get older, their brain cells die and are never replaced.

- The outside layer of the brain is gray in color. When people want you to think hard, they sometimes tell you to use your "gray matter."

- In the first part of an unborn baby's development, 250,000 neurons grow each minute. By the time the baby is born, she has almost all the neurons her brain will ever have.

- The animal with the biggest brain is the sperm whale. Its brain weighs more than 17 pounds (7.7 kilograms).

- Sleep gives the nervous system and the rest of the body a chance to rest. If you sleep eight hours each night and live to be 80 years old, you will be asleep for more than 26 years.

How to Learn More about the Nervous System

At the Library

Silverstein, Alvin, Virginia Silverstein, and Robert Silverstein.
The Nervous System.
New York: Twenty-First Century Books, 1997.

Simon, Seymour.
The Brain: Our Nervous System.
New York: Mulberry Books, 1999.

Stille, Darlene R.
The Nervous System.
Chicago: Children's Press, 1997.

On the Web

Visit our home page for lots of links about the nervous system:
http://www.childsworld.com/links.html
Note to Parents, Teachers, and Librarians: We routinely verify our
Web links to make sure they're safe, active sites—so encourage
your readers to check them out!

Through the Mail or by Phone

THE BRAIN INJURY ASSOCIATION OF AMERICA
105 North Alfred Street
Alexandria, VA 22314
800-444-6443
http://www.biausa.org

NATIONAL INSTITUTE OF MENTAL HEALTH
National Institutes of Health
6001 Executive Boulevard
Room 8184, MSC 9663
Bethesda, MD 20892-9663
301-443-4513
http://www.nimh.nih.gov

NATIONAL INSTITUTE OF NEUROLOGICAL DISORDERS AND STROKE
National Institutes of Health Neurological Institute
P.O. Box 5801
Bethesda, MD 20824
800-352-9424
http://www.ninds.nin.gov

Index

About the Author

Susan H. Gray has a bachelor's and a master's degree in zoology, and has taught college-level anatomy and physiology courses. In her 25 years as an author, she has written many medical articles, grant proposals, and children's books. Ms. Gray enjoys gardening, traveling, and playing the piano and organ. She has traveled twice to the Russian Far East to give organ workshops to church musicians. She also works extensively with American and Russian friends to develop medical and social service programs for Vladivostok, Russia. Ms. Gray and her husband, Michael, live in Cabot, Arkansas.